To Be the Difference

To Be the Difference

Poems

Willie James King

Press 53
Winston-Salem

Press 53, LLC
PO Box 30314
Winston-Salem, NC 27130

First Edition

Silver Concho Poetry Series
edited by Pamela Uschuk and William Pitt Root

Copyright © 2019 by Willie James King

All rights reserved, including the right of reproduction in whole or in part in any form except in the case of brief quotations embodied in critical articles or reviews. For permission, contact publisher at editor@Press53.com, or at the address above.

Cover design by Kevin Morgan Watson

Cover art, "These Waters Are for Everyone,"
Copyright © 2017 by William Pitt Root,
used by permission of the artist.

Author photograph by Andre Stephens Photography

Library of Congress Control Number
2018911958

Printed on acid-free paper
ISBN 978-1-941209-95-0

To
Cathy Smith Bowers
and
Colin Rand Kaepernick

In memory of my sister, Hattie-King Smith

Acknowledgments

Many thanks to the editors and staff at the following literary journals where select poems first appeared: *Cutthroat: A Journal of the Arts, New Contrast* (South Africa), *Kaleidoscope, Lunar Poetry* (UK), *The Long Islander: Walt's Corner, The Journal* (UK), *Jerry Jazz Musician, Rattle, Mobius: The Journal of Social Change, Malpais Review, and Truth To Power*, edited by Pam Uschuk.

Melanie Faith spent countless hours and much of her time helping me with this manuscript, offering much encouragement, in its early stages, for which I am especially grateful.

Thanks also to Jody Barnes, Robert Bharda, Suzanne Easterbrook, James Eret, Melanie Faith, Joel Griffith, Suzan Jantz, Patricia Spears Jones, Marilyn Kallet, Stellasue Lee, Al Maginnes, Antoinette Toni Lucas, Carter Monroe, and Robert Ward.

And with love to Kathryn Stripling Byer. Although she has left us, her impact on me and my work will never be forgotten.

Contents

I Went Home

I Went Home	3
A Love Poem in 14 Words	4
The Grass, the Rain	5
Mirrors	6
The Orange-striped One	7
Self-Autopsy of a Crazed Man	8
Grieve	9
I Will Not Forget	10
I Could Go on about These	11
My Country, Its People: Oh My God!	12
Always an Oddity	13
A Wall	14
Dolls, Gum, Bobby Socks	15
Seventeen	16
I'm the Boy	17
Dog-eared	18
Human	19

Another Dream

Mired	23
Love	24
But That Is for Another Dream	25
A Lure	26
No Doubt	27
He Doesn't Care	28
On Edge	29
The Rainbow	30
Not a Monarch	32
Desperate Measures	33
That's Okay	34
I Wish I Could	35
A Resurrection	36
To Be the Difference	37
Without Cause	38
Passion	39

The Part I've Not Written

Compassion	43
I Forget	44
Mind You	45

Above Raked Coals 46
A Pod of Pepper 47
Who You Are 48

Benediction

It Must Be Organic 51
Alone 52
Benediction 53
The Sun 54
The Trees 55
And Still 56
Sometimes 57
The Universe 58
Awkward Assurance 59

Author biography 61

I Went Home

The artist's role is to raise the consciousness of the people. To make them understand life, the world, and themselves more completely.
—Amiri Baraka

I Went Home

I spent time
in Selma today.
I returned home,
remembering,
and I am still
remembering

the lumber company
where father worked
as a de-barker

for over thirty years
without ever missing
a day. It took that long,
such persistence; then

the nursing home
where mother cared
for so many wasting away,
no different.

I drove back across
that infamous bridge
where gravity's
turgid undertow
brought tears,

the silent kind
no amount of sun
can cure,
no clearing
in sight.

I spent time
in Selma, today.
I went home.

A Love Poem in 14 Words

Much
depends
on a poet
with a new
pen, that
only he
must right.

The Grass, the Rain

The cows seem happy
to have their withered
blades of August grass
in this parched pasture
rain doesn't remember.

Today, a flag came down
from our capitol's dome,
where many are angry
and want to save a past
as if it were yet to happen.

It has, but it just couldn't last, as
so many things, unlike the grass,
the rain, are best remembered.

Mirrors

Got my fishing license
last week for days
like these. Nothing
is wrong with dreaming
of banking huge bass
even if some get thrown back.
I am tired of sick
folk screaming
to others as to
how they might feel better
or get well. See, mirrors
mean nothing anymore.

The Orange-Striped One

We got turbulent weather last night.
I went to my safe place, called the cats.
They came as their names were called,
that simple; snuggled close, dozed.
What scared me most is this:
they felt safe, I think, secure.
It hurts me that I couldn't save them
nor myself in the event of a tornado.
I felt so darn vulnerable,
even like a liar. Yet, they believed.
We'd go together. No other way,
no doubt. Small blessings. So far,
we are still here in our home
awaiting another round.
They know things: like, tonight,
the atmosphere is rife
primed for adventure.
Their eyes are upon me.
They don't stray. They still believe.
I just disturbed the youngest,
orange-striped one. Now
he is determined to claw onto my lap.
I will play hard for a while, but
I will yield. He, like the others,
knows he is loved. Unsaved.

Self-Autopsy of a Crazed Man

I was living through a breakdown
and didn't know it, had a good
job and just up and quit; a blue-
haze almost always hanging
about my head, making me wish
that I was dead. A man, wasted
by matters set forth by his own
hand, but I am still here. I rode
the storm alone, in a crisis that
must have caused Christ to
tremble at all of the terrible things
which I was tempted. All of those
pills, doctor bills, coupled with all
of those which kept my phone
ringing from hard-working collectors
persistent as the pain I couldn't pin
down with all of that pride which
caused me to keep the hurt inside
and couldn't make myself believe
I should seek some help I never
thought I'd need, before I broke
my own heart, and caused
too many others to bleed.

Grieve

Grass grins
at the blade.
It will grow
back again.
Grieve for
the mower.

I Will Not Forget

When my older siblings
walked out of school
to join the ranks of every other
youngster marching for freedom,
mere children witnessing
what no children should have
to witness, endure, like cattle prods,
teargas, sheriffs who had no care
for their wellbeing, I knew then,
as each day, my mom and dad
gathered us for prayer, to pray for them,
in case they never made it back
to us again. I remember.

It was a world divided then,
I saw white folk, and like them,
we all pretended not to see each other.
Thanks to my hardworking parents,
I didn't have to deal with them until
long after I had graduated from high
school, gone out into the world.
It was then that I witnessed racism.
But, by then, I had the heart of
an African King who had grown up
on another continent. My siblings
were awesome! I had that air
of arrogance, good, or bad, that
wouldn't allow me to be wounded
by them then, not even now.

I Could Go on about These

the lepers, ten of them
who went their way thinking
cures been about their skin
and scars, shame, afflictions

they thought were over and

done with. Imagine the Calvary
retracing its tracks from
the Trail of Tears, thinking
its travails over, won. But

history never hides crimes
it doesn't later expose, like
a child hiding from Hitler,
Jim Clark's time in Selma.

I could go on about these:
the Civil War. Lincoln? This
isn't what this poem's about,
but is: the dirty headlines:

Trials of King, of Rosa Parks.
Tested hearts are still hard.

Only one leper came back.

The Calvary isn't moved
concerning its past.

Each crime returns
to its perch, to rest.

A man is drowning
over there, calling, but
the life-guards don't
seem to care.

My Country, Its People: Oh My God!

For Obama, August 31, 2012

No matter
our trysts
and turns,
each day
is stained
by our own
sins: morning,
noon, night,
as evening's
colors blend,
the sun
becomes
unhinged,
darkness
becomes
our scourge,
it deepens,
as it swells, as if
it were meant
to last,
at least
until it
had its
chance
to litigate.

Always an Oddity

Always
an oddity,
anomaly.
Nothing
about me
was normal,
until you
entered
my life,
like poetry.

A Wall

But yours is the gift of Orpheus, sing,
I was told by someone whose words I trust,
which caused my pen to rise above the dust,
and to ruin a ream of bond paper again.

I write by hand, love the magic in this.
Go to New York! Others have told me, fine!
No matter where, I would have the same mind.
I must do it where I am, I insist.

If I were a parolee from prison,
with travel halted by periphery,
I'd still have the fire, the ability,
love that constantly fills me up with song.

Sometimes the right words can tear-down a wall,
a wall that had no true confines at all.

Dolls, Gum, Bobby Socks

Screw me if you want! Checkout my profile!
I read in an anonymous e-mail.
And I wondered: Money? Mania? When I
viewed a scantily clad girl's glad, sad eyes

(and sure, there was far much more to look at)
peering at the pic, her porno portal
at a world she could almost do without
while she swayed, undulated under light,

her dance, maniacal, more machine-like.
Someone will pay or attempt to buy her
(to seek his bliss from that disarmed angel),
while someone else might want to save her, spend
or borrow, if needed, to get her back,
the one who bought her dolls, gum, bobby socks.

Seventeen

Seventeen and she has seen more than some
sixty, it helps to know where she is from,
the baby her parents had aborted
because they were good people, respected.

What kind of child my baby might have been?
She asks herself from time to time, and then,
times when anyone is talking to her
their voice seems distant, far off, a mere blur.

Her parents wanted her to have the best
chance at life, saw her better than the rest.
They did not allow her to make that choice.
And now, she harkens to a fathom voice.

She speaks often to that unseen baby.
For this she's locked away, labeled: *Crazy*.

I'm the Boy

I'm the boy who was not conceived in love.
Two people screwed. I'm the one sentenced;
the one some want to rehabilitate;

that problem child! And, all of the above.
See, none of this happened by my consent.
What comes first: Re or to habilitate?

I don't know if I've done justice in jail;
or; well, if I should have been aborted.
How might I ever make sense of this?

Two kind folk who came down to pay my bail
said it was the school board that reported
how everything about me seems remiss?

Much of which might be true, more than maybe:
I've never been anybody's baby.

Dog-eared

No. Not ink
but my thumb print
on a dark paste
of a fly's remains
where it perched
upon the page.

And now that dirty
bastard's in my book,
as if the antagonist
needs a portrait.

The page's dog-eared
and the reading's
not quite done
lest I forget.

Human

There's
nothing
extraordinary
about being
human, but
to be.

Another Dream

Human progress is neither automatic nor inevitable...Every step toward the good of justice requires sacrifice, suffering, and struggle; the timeless exertions and passionate concern of dedicated individuals.
—Martin Luther King, Jr.

Mired

The weather is wild.
Tomorrow will be mild,
our warmest all week.
Tuesday, it might snow.
I take these as signs.
I am simply saying now:
Happy Birthday, Dr. King.
It won't get any better
than the world was when
you left. Let it go to hell
now. Ours isn't a racial ship.
I'd rather be left alone.
Dumb white folk will also
drown. It is sinking fast.
And, I no longer care.
What happened in Hawaii,
yesterday, just might be
a new normal. So be it.
America can deal with this
too. I have served her for
centuries, and she takes
without ever giving back.
Obama, it can't come-up
with an eraser capable
of obliterating your name.
And, I could care less if I
am condemned or con-
doned for writing this. I have
PTSD, from having served,
and PTSD from what I don't
deserve. Tell me, how long
must a man remain mired?
I won't. I don't do dinners.
I'd rather be left alone.

Love

There is
sufficient
evidence
that when
someone
loves you,
they just
won't leave
you alone.

But That Is for Another Dream

I crawled from the comfort of half-
a-century quilts, hit the lamp switch,
pulled out a bundle of rejection slips
from the top drawer of the bureau

by the headboard of my bed and searched
through each passionately, one-by-one
hoping there might have been just one
I missed. Outside, it was raining lambs

and lions. I had read them right. I rebound them
and set them down regretful respect,
eased back into bed, turned off the soft lamp light,
then pulled the quilts about the nape of my neck.

And I sought sleep in those old, worn,
raisin-like hands that had sewn them.
I could almost smell the odor of camphor
it seemed, but that is for another dream.

A Lure

Turtles on the torpid trunks of felled trees,
where ripples raise the back of the river,
save for when a calmness arrests the breeze
here where the earth's a constant giver.

The kingfisher does not err when it dives
nor the sunrays that grace the hill's agate
glaring brightly as if the hill has eyes
as if every rock and stone's awake.

Less interested in angling as before,
I search the sandbars for antler-like drift
beautiful as what some slay a deer for
cheaper than what might be found among thrift.

But I cannot speak as in my heart's pure,
when what brought me here was to cast a lure.

No Doubt

Jan. 14, 2018,
in California
a church was dis-
mantled by rain
and mudslide
today, so to say,
splintered, save
for its crucifix
lavished by light
that had been
hidden too long,
no doubt. Truth
immutable.

He Doesn't Care

It is cold out, but he doesn't care,
warmth is hard to find anywhere
sense is just a silly subject,
and a broke man has no budget;
curse is a hard life to heir.

He only has himself to compare,
dumped, he is also given a dare;
still, he rides the waves of reject.
It is cold out, but he doesn't care.

The steely eyes of loathers stare,
not wanting him to find his fare,
and although the world might do that,
cold, he stands still, does not fidget;
nothing lasts, he wants to be there.
It is cold out, but he doesn't care.

On Edge

It stuns me when folk think
America is in a terrible condition
worse than ever before. Imagine,
four-hundred years of slavery, and
it exists now, if you are attentive,
you can see. Imagine having
to be separated from your family,
as family meant nothing then
when there was a Trump behind
every hedge, tree, ready to lop
off the limb of an attempted escapee,
those singing praise songs of hope
to no avail but a noose, shotgun blast,
dogs and horses trained on them,
none like what occurred in Selma,
wearing the same old cotton-
smelly clothes, day-in, day-out. You
think these are scary times now. When
all that matters to you, concerns you,
when one's life does not depend
on the end-of-the world. It depends
on now! Folk grow numb daily
dealing with bullshit, bigotry, who'd
rather give up all before bending
to kiss one's ass like politicians, per se.
I am not bothered in the least bit by none
of this absurdity. How long can one exist
in a state of being alarmed? Remember
those horrible accounts of our Civil War?
Remember the Indians, their travails?
Things fester, come to a head. Trump
and Ben Carson both are as American-made
as can be. Sometimes, I equate the tales
of slaves to what cops are doing now.
Are there different manifestations
of terrorism? If so, please,
would someone name them? This
is merely seeking what I would
like to know, now that it seems
that everyone's life is on edge.

The Rainbow

It is no wonder,
just the way it is
heading home,

approaching that
iron-clad bridge
Edmund Pettus

as I feel its pull,
its tug, its blue-
gray muscle of

wandering water,
like a magnet, its
cold hold on me.

From mid-mount
I look down on a
small sunken city

still divided where
people, dazed,
pass in and out,

around, through
each other, as if
unaware, unamazed,

not seeing beyond,
not willing to, but
behind, seeking to

hold-on to a past
they're longing to return,
find a path back to

is why I never desire
to kiss the ground on
arriving, anymore, nor

being among them,
their brass hearts, iron
minds of murmur. He's

a King, reckon he's kin
to Martin's approach. I
am kin to humanity.

The last time I was
leaving there I saw
it arched to my right,

over the river, huge,
hallowed. I wondered
why most would want

to see its sign without
ever believing they can
become the rainbow.

Not a Monarch

Someday, we'll appear
petrified in our places
as those old Egyptians.
Nothing has changed.

Desperate Measures

It is always about now, not the hour;
so much can happen in a split second,
the car stalls, or someone makes a wrong turn
and all that's left is meat meshed with metal.

Suddenly the earth opens, buildings sink.
The odor of rot helps to find those dead.
Someone went back for his dog or his cat;
and Lord, don't let it be for a loved one.

After a three-year stint in the army,
I thought I could live peaceably without
any thought of killing. But, when a man
kidnaps a boy, holds him in a bunker,
especially a kid who's his, or not,
even if I had to pull out my hair
to the root once done, I could kill.

That's Okay

You know how sometimes our bodies aren't ours,
how they can belong to a grieving breeze
or mornings when it is too brisk, or cold
disobedient, when we become old,

when others want silence, we choose to sneeze.
Through like testimonials and trials,
we are like the unfolding of a scroll,
gentle, kind, at first, then later we seethe.

Today, I went down to that old, dried well
and stared at sand that gives no reflection,
saw a doll's twisted face, so full of hell
like mine, facing closed doors, or deception.

Haul me out of this pit, she seemed to say.
Should you decide to leave me, that's okay.

I Wish I Could

I love the sound of rain
and it is raining nonstop.
I have drawn the blinds
so I can look out at our
wet, wintry weather. All
three cats are kneeling,
side by side, before the
hearth flames. I can re-
call my father's booming
voice: What!? Are you try-
ing to warm the world!?
Tonight, I wish I could.

A Resurrection

I walked
the yard
this morning
with my first
cup. I saw
the perennials
are putting-out
green, gold shoots,
especially the
roses cut back
last fall. I felt
like them,
determined
in all this rain
continuing warmth,
knowing it will
soon be spring,
a resurrection
of so many
seemingly
dead things
that didn't
give up.

To Be the Difference

I used a plastic grocery bag
to place the fledgling starling
back in its nest at the top of
the cavernous brick column
of my car-porch. And I did, at least
in spite of its over-alarmed parents,
shouting aspersions. They saw me as a threat
regardless, even though they chose to
build so close to my door.

Maybe it was the night lights that drew them
near. Something I will never know.
As its frail body fought hard for life,
I felt the strain of my years
and did what a human does who
feels convicted to care for small
lives that don't depend on us,
left to their limited choice.
I felt compelled to be the difference.
And not just because it was a bird,
Nigerian girls are no less important.

Without Cause

A third frost has occurred
and the collards are huge,
still growing, leaves open.
And, every colony within
or upon their green stems
seems to prosper, celebrating *cold*.
So am I. I pulled an overcoat
from my closet; I never thought
after three years it would get
to kiss my ashen skin again.
I was a brown bear today,
gloves covering my frigid paws,
matching scarf about my neck.
I'm no lover of winter. It's its time,
and I am glad to see it's arrived.
The oxymoron is its brilliant sun,
stellar cold. I endure knowing
it does not overcome fall
each year without cause.

Passion

An acceptance? Seldom.
You should see the rejections
in the bureau by my bed.

The Part I've Not Written

The future rewards those who press on. I don't have time to feel sorry for myself, I don't have time to complain. I'm going to press on.
—President Barack Obama

Compassion

I don't celebrate
nor sing myself.
I would not leave
you absent
of song.

I Forget

There is a reading in which
I am invited to participate,
no one I know knew I am
a poet. All of that's changed
now that my family, friends
and neighbors are aware.

Think I might have said so
here or there, but I only feel
like one when I, please ex-
cuse this, am poeting, then.
See, I am a father, uncle,
brother, neighbor, gardener,
activist, friend, individual,
loner, all else, like bill-maker,
bill-payer, prayer, sinner,
purveyor, painter, crooner,
pruner, PTSD VET. And,
something else, I forget.

Mind You

It seems
that people
who are brought
together by poetry
seldom part;
mind you, I
said seldom.

Above Raked Coals

She's a camel in a sage, cashmere coat
basking in July sun near the window.
"I am cold," she says; then, she clears her throat.
Her blood is like sump: thick and slow to flow.

"Will you turn on some heat?" she asks. The room
temperature is at seventy-eight.
She grapples with her sluggish mind, with gloom.
"You think Joey is going to be late?"

She is my mom. I don't know who he is.
Death, perhaps? Or a still-born before me?
I tell her, "I think so," give her more pills.
"Momma, we will just have to wait and see."

All day, every day, is how this goes.
My soul is a cobweb above raked coals.

A Pod of Pepper

I thought the tomato was red
until I placed a pod of pepper
beside it. I looked into the distance
onto a trellis of trees and noticed
none of their greens were alike.

They vary, at best, as one might
stare at a myriad of black faces
while trying, in earnest,
to single out a suspect.

Who You Are

I love the ping pong
of words, as when
they are pretty, nicely
lettered upon a page.
But damn a dossier.
Come, sit and chat
with me, so that I might
find out who you are.

Benediction

*Just living is not enough. . .One must have sunshine,
freedom, and a little flower.*
—Hans Christian Andersen

It Must Be Organic

I cannot dredge the depths of what I do.
That would be like arguing against art,
the point where form and conjecture construe.
This is, to me, the most important part.

I can't participate in what I make
than the moon crossing the sky in its turn,
or night and day on their axis rotate.
I'm the scar that is left after the burn.

It's not my wish to will or impose—
It happens: the artifices not controlled
no matter how much I want to compose.
It must be organic. It must implode,

must materialize out of thin air.
Then I am awed by what's suddenly there.

Alone

A bolt of late-
evening sun
fills the loft.
It's nice not
being alone.

Benediction

The praying
mantis that's pressed
against my window-
pane is neither
bad nor good.

The Sun

The sun is angling
in an august manner,
it will form a gorgeous mantle
above the trees before it melts.
Days like these, I don't care to
ever forget. There might be
some magenta, but no matter,
I am certain, this day's end
will be dramatically beautiful,
give me hope for tomorrow.
Oh, any thought of politics,
people, are lost in this.
Isn't nature grand?
Ultimately, isn't it
all there is?

The Trees

Last year I said: I won't cut them down,
the two Bradford pear trees on my front lawn.
They begin to drop their leaves in August,
which continues long after October's
over. So, I mulch some with the mower,
use the blower, and often an old rake.
I have flowers planted above their roots.
I forgive them as I forgive some folk.
A tree is just a tree, but I have lived
too long among people who're imperfect
to cut down a couple of trees, as if
they are mean, trifling, ruled by malice.
I pick up beer cans, popcorn bags daily,
and other things I do not wish to name.
The trees may not know it isn't autumn;
they are not ruthless, crass, nor insane.

And Still

I remember my mother
when I look at old poems
then ask: How in the hell
did I let you leave home
looking like that? Poet as
parent, I guess, tired one
at best, raising the brood,
brooding the raised, uh?
and still sending them out.

Sometimes

Sometimes, a man
who is wide-eyed
needs to be tender
and kind to himself
at the end of a long
awesome day. He
needs to point out
the cottons nearby
for bed on a cool
night, say: it is time
you shave, shower,
in love, as he'd say
to his, or to any
other child; he needs
to be strong enough
to pull the sheets up
snug about his neck
while he awaits an
old song that's almost
remembered to take
on a life of its own
as it does most nights
when he depends on it
to rock him to sleep.

The Universe

I've seen
how the laws
of the universe
work against
man's; and,
I'm thankful.

Awkward Assurance

A bay-breasted warbler soared in
then it settled on a flimsy branch
of the crape myrtle's new growth
where its balance seemed clumsy

at first, out of sorts, before it began its song,
far bigger than its tiny body will ever be,
like a person who is paid to appease, like
someone correcting an unfavorable incident
until it suddenly shook itself loose and flew

through stout green limbs of sycamore,
fiercely tunneling toward the late sunlight
in acrobatic grace, awkward assurance,
as if it had others scheduled too.

Willie James King was born and reared in Orrville, Alabama. He holds an MFA from Queens University of Charlotte and has published several books including *The House in the Heart* (2007) and *Autumn's Only Blood* (2013), both from Tebot Bach Press. His poems have appeared widely in such publications as *America*, *Appalachian Heritage*, *Confrontation*, *Cutthroat, A Journal of the Arts*, *New Contrast* (South Africa), *English Journal*, *Rattle*, *Southern Poetry Review*, and *Urthona* (UK). He has nine Pushcart Prize nominations and one Best of the Net. He resides in Montgomery, Alabama.

www.ingramcontent.com/pod-product-compliance
Lightning Source LLC
LaVergne TN
LVHW041346080426
835512LV00006B/635